Hide-and-Seek Prince

2 Kings 11:1–12:16
(Joash)

Mary Manz Simon

Illustrated by Dennis Jones

CPH®
SAINT LOUIS

For Eldon Meyer
Mark 16:15

Books by Mary Manz Simon from Concordia Publishing House

Hear Me Read Level 1 Series
What Next?
Drip Drop
Jibber Jabber
Hide the Baby
Toot! Toot!
Bing!
Whoops!
Send a Baby
A Silent Night
Follow That Star
Row the Boat
Rumble, Rumble
Who Will Help?
Sit Down
Come to Jesus
Too Tall, Too Small
Hurry, Hurry!
Where Is Jesus?

Hear Me Read Big Books Series
What's Next?
Drip Drop
Send a Baby

Follow That Star
Sit Down
Come to Jesus
Too Tall, Too Small
Where Is Jesus?

Hear Me Read Level 2 Series
The No-Go King
Hurray for the Lord's Army!
The Hide-and-Seek Prince
Daniel and the Tattletales
The First Christmas
Through the Roof
A Walk on the Waves
Thank You, Jesus

Little Visits® Series
Little Visits on the Go
Little Visits for Toddlers
Little Visits with Jesus
Little Visits Every Day

Stop! It's Christmas
God's Children Pray
My First Diary

Copyright © 1994 Concordia Publishing House
3558 S. Jefferson Avenue, St. Louis, MO 63118-3968
Manufactured in the United States of America

Library of Congress Cataloging in Publication Data

Simon, Mary Manz, 1948–
       The hide-and-seek prince: II Kings 11–12:16: Joash / Mary Manz Simon; illustrated by Dennis Jones.
              p.   cm.   — (Hear me read. Level 2)
       ISBN 0-570-04740-4
       1. Bible stories, English—O.T. Kings, 2nd. 2. Joash, King of Judah—Juvenile literature. 3. Bible. O.T. Kings, 2nd, XI–XII, 16—Biography—Juvenile literature. [1. Joash, King of Judah. 2. Bible stories—O.T.] I. Jones, Dennis, ill. II Title. III. Title: Joash. IV. Series: Simon, Mary Manz, 1948– Hear me read. Level 2.

BS580.J48S55 1994
222'.5409505—dc20   93-35606

03 04 05 06 07 08 09 10 11 12   09 08 07 06 05 04 03 02 01 00

Long ago a woman became queen.
She was a wicked queen.

The wicked queen wanted to kill
someone.
She wanted to kill a little prince.
Prince Joash was just a baby.

"Soldiers, find Joash," said the wicked
queen.
"Find that little prince," she said.
"He must not escape.
Joash must not grow up to be king."

The queen's soldiers raced out of
the palace.
The soldiers raced past the temple.
The soldiers raced through the city.

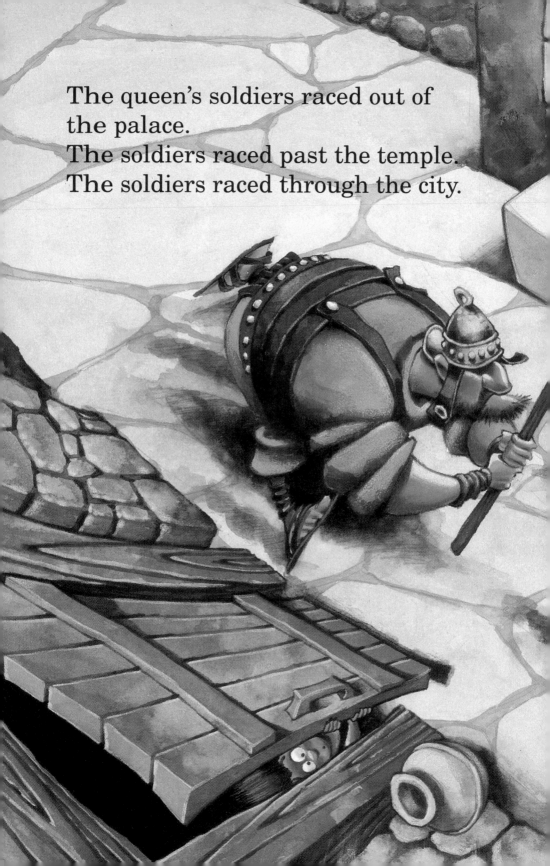

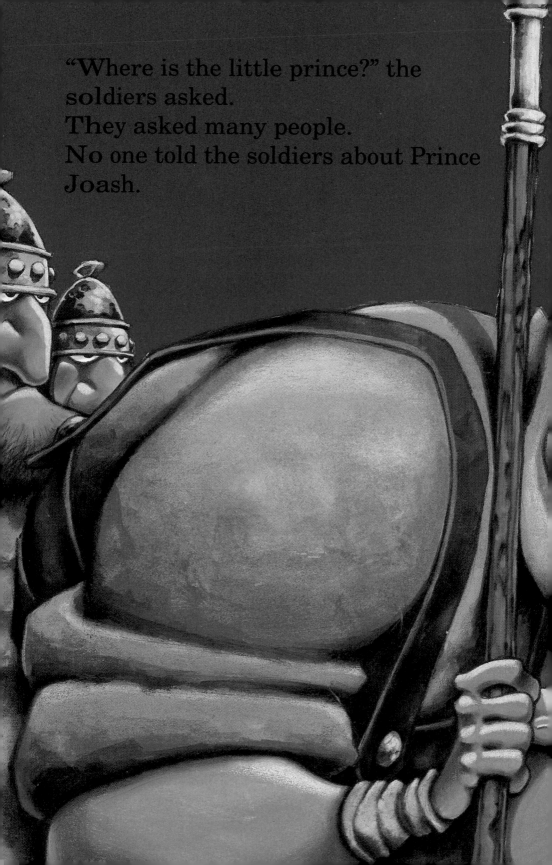

"Where is the little prince?" the
soldiers asked.
They asked many people.
No one told the soldiers about Prince
Joash.

No one told them about the little prince.

"We must hide baby Joash," said his aunt.
"We must hide baby Joash so he can grow up to be king."

"Where is a hiding place?" asked the priest.
"Where is a secret hiding place?"

"Here," said his aunt.
"We can hide little Joash here in the temple.
The soldiers will not find little Joash.
They will not find little Joash here."

The soldiers were still looking
for Joash.

"Where is the little prince?"
they asked.
No one told them about the secret
hiding place.

The wicked queen sent more soldiers.
"Find that little prince," she said.

The soldiers looked and looked.
The soldiers did not find the little
prince.

Joash was in the secret hiding place.
God kept Joash safe.

A year went by.
Baby Joash was growing up.

Another year went by.

"How long must Joash stay in the secret hiding place?" his aunt asked. "How long must we hide Joash?"

"We must hide Prince Joash so he can grow up to be king," said the priest. "God will help us keep Joash safe."

Little Prince Joash grew and grew.
He stayed in his secret hiding place.

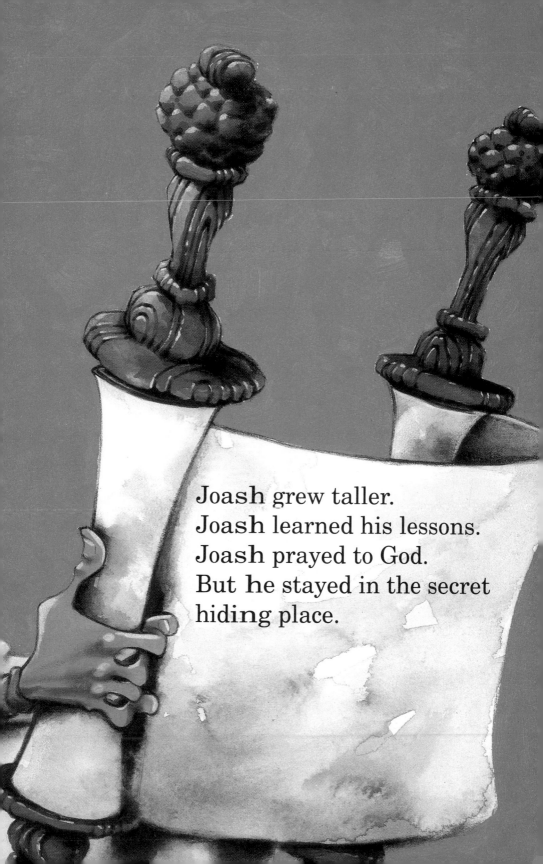

Joash grew taller.
Joash learned his lessons.
Joash prayed to God.
But he stayed in the secret
hiding place.

"Now," said the priest one day.
"Now Joash can be king."
Prince Joash was seven years old.

The priest walked out to the streets.
"Come to the temple," he called.
Many people came to the temple.

The priest walked through the city.
"Come to the temple," he called.
Even more people came to the temple.

Many people came to the temple.
The priest put a crown on Joash's head.
The people were happy to see their new king.

"Long live the king," said the people.
"Long live King Joash," the people shouted.

The wicked queen heard all the noise.
She rushed from the palace.
She rushed to the temple.
She looked at all the people.

"What are all these people doing here?" shouted the wicked queen. "What is all this noise?"

"Soldiers, soldiers, capture the wicked
queen!" said the priest.
"She must not escape.
Arrest the wicked queen.
Joash is our new king."

The priest helped the little king.
Joash grew and grew.
He was a good king.
Joash prayed to God.
God kept Joash safe.

The wicked queen had let the temple
fall apart.
Joash fixed the temple.

The wicked queen had told the people to
pray to false gods.
Now Joash and the people prayed to
the true God.

"Long live the king!" shouted
the people.
"Long live King Joash!"

Joash thanked God.
Joash thanked God for the priest who
had helped him.
Joash thanked God for his aunt who
had helped him hide.
Joash thanked God for his secret hiding
place.

"Thank You, God!" said Joash.

About the Author
Mary Manz Simon holds a doctoral degree in education with a specialty in early childhood education. She has taught at levels from preschool through postgraduate. Dr. Simon is the best-selling author of more than 40 children's books, including *Little Visits with Jesus*. She and her husband, the Reverend Henry A. Simon, are the parents of three children.